365 inspiring bib   .fe

a little daily wisdom

joel fotinos & august gold

PARACLETE PRESS

BREWSTER, MASSACHUSETTS

A Little Daily Wisdom: 365 Inspiring Bible Verses to Change Your Life

Copyright © 2009 by Joel Fotinos and August Gold

ISBN 978-1-55725-648-5

Copyright notices for the Bible versions used in this edition are listed on the "Permissions" page at the end of the book.

Library of Congress Cataloging-in-Publication Data
Bible. English. Selections. 2010.
  A little daily wisdom : 365 inspiring Bible verses to change your life / compiled by Joel Fotinos and August Gold.
      p. cm.
  ISBN 978-1-55725-648-5 (french flaps, deckled edge, pbk.)
  1. Devotional calendars. 2. Bible--Devotional literature. I. Fotinos, Joel. II. Gold, August, 1955- III. Title.
  BS390.L58 2010
  220.5'208--dc22   2009043481

10   9   8   7   6   5   4   3   2   1

All rights reserved. No portion of this book may be reproduced, stored in an electronic retrieval system, or transmitted in any form or by any means—electronic, mechanical, photocopy, recording, or any other—except for brief quotations in printed reviews, without the prior permission of the publisher.

Published by Paraclete Press
Brewster, Massachusetts
www.paracletepress.com

Printed in the United States of America

contents

Introduction • v

january

february

march

april

may

june

july

august

september

october

november

december

My Favorite Verses • 369

Translation Guide • 370

Permissions • 374

introduction

Letting the Bible Change Your Life

Several years ago, I was working in a job in San Francisco that was, to say the least, unsettling. The corporation that owned our company was in the midst of several rounds of lay-offs—in less than two years, we had gone from a staff of over 200 people to now just 40. Morale was low, and each day every staff member would wonder if this was the day they would get laid off.

I clearly remember one morning, as I was on the bus going to my job feeling depressed and scared, a thought suddenly came to my mind: *all things work together for good to those who love God.* It was a Bible verse I had memorized years earlier and hadn't thought about since, and yet, here it was, right when I needed those very words. I immediately felt better, gained strength from this Bible promise, and faced my day with new strength—or, I should say, using God's strength as my own. I repeated it throughout that day, and the days that followed, and what once had been a difficult, dark time became a spiritual quest that brought me closer to God.

I decided to memorize more Bible verses. In fact, the more Bible verses I memorized, the more they "spontaneously" would pop up in my mind, seemingly at the very moment that I needed them most. I came to realize that memorizing Bible verses was like taking spiritual vitamins. Vitamins are supplements we take in order to improve our health and give us more well-being. We don't usually see results of the vitamins on the first day we take them, and their positive effect may be subtle, occurring over a long period of time. Likewise, memorizing Bible verses—our spiritual vitamins—may or may not profoundly affect our lives the day we memorize the verse. But like good vitamins, they stay in our system, providing nutrients and help as we need it. And then, no matter what happens in our lives, these verses will provide comfort, strength, and joy.

We've designed *A Little Daily Wisdom: 365 Inspiring Bible Verses to Change Your Life* so that you can begin using it immediately. The verses are nearly all short, inspiring, easy to memorize, and every book of the Bible is represented. In some cases, we've taken just a portion of a verse or a paragraph, pulling out the essential message so that it is easier to memorize. We looked up each verse in the nine translations we used, to find the one that had the clearest message. Since the purpose of this book is specifically to uplift you and to help you in memorizing the words, feel free to let these verses lead you back to the Bible for deeper study and to see each verse in its fullness and in context. You can use this book, then, as a powerful supplement to your life, and allow it to nourish and uplift you.

Try to begin each day with this book, spending a few moments learning that day's Bible verse. Read it several times, and even read it aloud. Read it with feeling. Close your eyes and repeat it until you feel you can remember it. For each verse, you may want to ask yourself some questions that will help you to internalize the verse you've read.

What does the verse say to me?
How is it applicable in my life?
How does the verse make me feel?

Throughout the day, repeat this verse over and over to yourself so that you can stay present in its promise. You might even take this book with you, or, if that isn't handy, you may want to write out the verse on a card or a Post-it Note and keep it where you can see if over and over.

You'll find that certain verses stick in your mind immediately, that their message is one you need right away. Other verses that you memorize won't be as obvious in their connection to your life—but memorize these verses anyway. A time may come when one of these very verses can offer you its help and hope.

After each Bible verse is included a daily affirmative prayer, which is a way to activate the power of the verse in your life. As you memorize the verse, use the prayer then to seal the promise of the verse between you and God. Memorizing the verses and then following it up with a prayer will, if you let it, have a profound impact in your life. And there are even pages at the end where you can write in your own favorite verses.

So begin your journey today. Memorize your first Bible verse, and begin this new habit that can and will yield amazing results in your life. Think of each new verse you memorize as another vitamin that will bring health and energy to your spiritual life. And allow the many promises of God to become true and present for you.

a little daily wisdom

· january 1 ·

So God created man in his own image, in the image of God he created him; male and female he created them. And God blessed them.

—

GENESIS 1:27–28A

Today I give thanks to God for creating me.

· january 2 ·

2007~ redo "nursery + bedroom into Scraping room

I will present to God a tenth
of everything he gives me.

—

GENESIS 28:22B

Today I give back to God, with gratitude.

Do good for good is good to do!

january 3

I will not let You go unless You bless me.

—

GENESIS 32:26B

Today I find the blessing in everything in my life.

God has been very gracious to me.
I have more than enough.

—

GENESIS 33:11B

Today I am grateful for all that I have.

enroute to Tulip Way~

january 5

1998 ~ on Route 103 a golden sun, peeking over trees, bathed the area in a golden foggy glow as fog laid down a blanket over the earth this morning

> You meant evil against me;
> but God meant it for good.
>
> GENESIS 50:20B

Today I realize that everything that happened to me can bless me.

2003 ~ Today Zachary said "bird" to the TV and then pointed to hanging hummingbirds and repeated 'bird'.

• january 6 •

The Lord answered, "Who makes people able to speak or makes them deaf or unable to speak? Who gives them sight or makes them blind? Don't you know that I am the one who does these things? Now go! When you speak, I will be with you and give you the words to say."

—

EXODUS 4:11–12

Today I let go and let God speak through me.

1973 ~ Jeffrey Parker Watson born in La Mesa, CA

· january 7 ·

Don't be afraid! Be brave, and you will see the
Lord save you today.

—

EXODUS 14:13B

To choose doubt as a philosophy of life is akin to choosing immobility as a means of transportation. ~ The Life of Pi

Today I will be brave in my faith.

· january 8 ·

1991 ~ Meghan Lea Case
Tuesday 3:50 pm

God will direct you, you will be able to endure.

—

EXODUS 18:23A

Today I believe in divine guidance, and follow where it leads.

2007 ~ to Homestead, Fl
re panther project
(Elderhostel)

My presence will go with you,
and I will give you rest.

—

Exodus 33:14

2004 ~ w/ Jane to Baja, CA, Mexico
to watch whales ~ and to
Copper Canyon –

Today I rest in the divine peace of God.

You shall be holy,
for I the Lord your God am holy.

—

LEVITICUS 19:2B

Today I am in complete unity with God the Good.

1995~ Crystal River via Jacksonville, F
swim w/ manatees

A tithe of everything from the land, whether grain from the soil or fruit from the trees, belongs to the Lord; it is holy to the Lord.

—

LEVITICUS 27:30

Today I give to God, knowing God returns what I give tenfold.

The Lord bless you and keep you; the Lord make his face shine upon you and be gracious to you; the Lord turn his face toward you and give you peace.

—

Numbers 6:24–26

Today good flows through me to all that I come in contact with.

2001 ~ Vegas (time share) by Jane
and Susan Nolan

· january 13 ·

Love the Lord your God with all your heart and
with all your soul and with all your strength.

—

DEUTERONOMY 6:5

Today God shines through my thoughts and my actions.

Always remember that it is the Lord your God
who gives you power to become rich.

—

DEUTERONOMY 8:18A

Today I know I am rich in the love of God.

Be strong and courageous!
Do not be afraid of them!
The Lord your God will go ahead of you.
He will neither fail you nor forsake you.

—

DEUTERONOMY 31:6

Do all the good you can
By all the means you can
In all the ways you can
In all the places you can
At all the times you can
To all the people you can
As long as ever you can.
                    John Wesley

Today I am strong and courageous.

Whatever you have commanded us we will do,
and wherever you send us we will go.

—

JOSHUA 1:16

Today the Spirit within me makes my way clear and easy.

You know with all your heart and soul that not one of all the good promises the Lord your God gave you has failed. Every promise has been fulfilled; not one has failed.

—

JOSHUA 23:14B

Today I believe God's holy promises to me.

But as for me and my house,
we will serve the Lord.

—

JOSHUA 24:15c

Grace ~ the freely given
unmerited favor and
love of God.
~ the influence or Spirit of
God, operating in man.
~ moral strength

Today I will serve the Lord in all that I do.

2002: Zachary's 1st laugh!

• january 19 •

Go assured. God's looking out for you all the way.

—

JUDGES 18:6

He who learns must suffer
And even in our sleep
Pain that cannot forget
Falls drop by drop upon the heart
And in our own despair
against our will
comes wisdom to us
by the awful grace of God.

Aeschylus 525-456 BC
Greek poet & dramatist

Today I carry God's assurances with me.

Where you go, I will go.
Where you live, I will live.
Your people will be my people,
and your God will be my God.

—

RUTH 1:16B

Today I know that God is always faithful.

2011 ~ to Canaan Valley, West Va ~ to ski
w/ Melanie & family, Mark Case & family
and Nathan

· january 21 ·

You make me strong and happy, Lord.

—

1 SAMUEL 2:1A

Today I am happy in the Lord.

Because of your promise, and according to your own heart, you have brought about all this greatness.

—

2 Samuel 7:21

Today my mind rejoices in certainty and in God's assurances.

Carolyn Morrison Lewis
11-02-1938 ~ 01-22-1998
of colon cancer

Yου are great, O Lord God. For there is none like you, and there is no God besides you.

—

2 SAMUEL 7:22A

Today I have no other gods before God.

The Lord is my rock, my fortress, and my savior;
my God is my rock, in whom I find protection.

—

2 SAMUEL 22:2–3A

Grief can't be shared.
Everyone carries it alone,
his own way,
his own burden.
Anne Morrow Lindbergh

Today God is my rock and my protection.

O Lord, you are my lamp.
The Lord turns my darkness into light.

—

2 Samuel 22:29

Today I see everything with the light of God.

The Spirit of the Lord speaks through me;
his words are upon my tongue.

—

2 SAMUEL 23:2

Today the spirit of the Lord speaks through me.

2003 - Thank You, God, for knowing that happiness comes from within (You!).

· january 27 ·

What do you want? Ask, and I will give it to you!

—

1 KINGS 3:5B

2006 ~ to Charleston, SC for wedding of Jamie to Frank Kerr. on 01-28 w/ Mark Case, Melanie, Kelly & Stephanie -

Today I ask for and receive what I need and want.

The Lord has promised
there will be more than enough.

—

2 KINGS 4:43B

Today I believe that all I ask for will be given me, and even more.

Praise the Lord because he is good to us, and his love never fails.

—

1 CHRONICLES 16:34

Today God's love fills my life.

Both riches and honor come from you,
and you rule over all.

—

1 CHRONICLES 29:12A

1998 Joel retires ~@ age 59 after 36 years & 8 months !

Today God's riches and honor shine through me.

O Lord our God, all this abundance that we have provided for building you a house for your holy name comes from your hand and is all your own.

—

1 Chronicles 29:16

Today I realize that God is my only source.

No one can ever build a temple large enough for God—even the heavens are too small a place for him to live in!

—

2 CHRONICLES 2:6A

Today I let my life be a temple for the Lord.

I was encouraged because the Lord my God
was helping me.

—

Ezra 7:28

Today my courage comes from God within.

Be quiet, for this day is holy; do not be grieved.

—

NEHEMIAH 8:11B

Today is holy, and I am quiet in it.

2007
Charles
"Chuck" dies!
Brown

· february 4 ·

It could be that you were made . . .
for a time like this!

—

ESTHER 4:14B

2000 ~ To ZION National Park
in Utah w/ Joel, Jane,
and Susan Nolan!

Today I realize that I am where I am for a reason.

• february 5 •

Carmi Lou Grissett Watson
02/05/12 ~ 11/28/71

We hear with our ears, taste with our tongues, and gain some wisdom from those who have lived a long time. But God is the real source of wisdom and strength.

—

JOB 12:11–13

Today God is my strength and my wisdom.

Chuck Brown
1927 - 2007

2007 – w/ Bobbi Farr to AC, NJ

· february 6 ·

Surrender to God All-Powerful!
You will find peace and prosperity.

—

JOB 22:21

Today I surrender everything to the Divine.

The Spirit of God has made me, and the breath
of the Almighty gives me life.

—

JOB 33:4

2004 ~ To Big Sky, Montana
w/ Mark, Karen, Kris & Andie
plus Burkes

Today I breathe with the breath of Life.

God gives each of us chance after chance to be . . .
brought into the light that gives life.

—

JOB 33:29–30

*2014 ~ w/ Joel to Death Valley
N.P. and Vegas
for 2 weeks*

Today I live my life in God's light.

Be silent, and I will teach you wisdom.

—

JOB 33:33B

Today I realize that everything is beautiful and meaningful.

They delight in doing everything the Lord wants; day and night they think about his law. They are like trees planted along the riverbank, bearing fruit each season without fail. Their leaves never wither, and in all they do, they prosper.

—

PSALM 1:2–3

Today I delight in everything the Lord asks of me.

You are a shield around me, O Lord; you bestow glory on me and lift up my head. To the Lord I cry aloud, and he answers me from his holy hill.

—

PSALM 3:3–4

Today God protects and guides me.

· february 12 ·

Answer me when I call, O God who declares me
innocent. Take away my distress. Have mercy on
me and hear my prayer.

—

PSALM 4:1

Today I know the mercy of God, and I am innocent.

I can lie down and sleep soundly because you,
Lord, will keep me safe.

—

PSALM 4:8

Today the safety of God surrounds me.

Because of your great mercy, I come to your house, Lord, and I am filled with wonder as I bow down to worship at your holy temple. You do what is right, and I ask you to guide me.

—

PSALM 5:7–8A

Today I see good in everything, and God's love manifested in every event.

· february 15 ·

When I look at your heavens, the work of your fingers, the moon and the stars, which you have set in place, what is man that you are mindful of him?

—

PSALM 8:3-4A

Today I am reminded of how awesome is God's creation.

The words of the Lord are pure words, like silver tried in a furnace of earth, purified seven times.

—

PSALM 12:6

Today I listen to the pure words of the Lord.

Thank You, God, for this day

· february 17 ·

I trust your love, and I feel like celebrating because
you rescued me. You have been good to me, Lord,
and I will sing about you.

—

PSALM 13:5–6

a copy of these verses, along
with a book, "Celebration of
Miracles" by Jodie Berndt,
sent to Jane Stern today

Today I sing the praises of God.

You, Lord, are all I want! You are my choice, and you keep me safe. You make my life pleasant, and my future is bright.

—

PSALM 16:5–6

Today I choose God above all else.

• february 19 •

I praise you, Lord, for being my guide. Even in the darkest night, your teachings fill my mind. I will always look to you, as you stand beside me and protect me from fear.

—

PSALM 16:7–8

Today I know that God is always with me.

I am your chosen one. You have shown me the path
to life, and you make me glad by being near to me.
Sitting at your right side, I will always be joyful.

—

PSALM 16:10A, 11

2003

Today, see Mt Ranier
from the air
from the road
from the field!

Also, a truly incredible
West Coast Rainbow - Vibrant!

Today I joyfully walk down the path of Life.

You alone are God! Only you are a mighty rock. You give me strength and guide me right. You make my feet run as fast as those of a deer, and you help me stand on the mountains.

—

PSALM 18:31–33

Today my strength is in the Lord alone.

The Lord is my shepherd; I shall not want. He makes me to lie down in green pastures; He leads me beside the still waters. He restores my soul; He leads me in the paths of righteousness for His name's sake.

—

PSALM 23:1–3

Today I know that the Lord is my shepherd.

Yea, though I walk through the valley of the shadow of death, I will fear no evil; for You are with me; Your rod and Your staff, they comfort me.

—

PSALM 23:4

Today I fear nothing.

You prepare a table before me in the presence of my enemies; You anoint my head with oil; my cup runs over. Surely goodness and mercy shall follow me all the days of my life; and I will dwell in the house of the Lord forever.

—

PSALM 23:5–6

Today I live the life God asks of me.

Who may ascend into the hill of the Lord?
Or who may stand in His holy place?
He who has clean hands and a pure heart.

—

PSALM 24:3–4A

Today I let go of anything that is not clean or pure.

I offer you my heart, Lord God, and I trust you.
Show me your paths and teach me to follow;
guide me by your truth and instruct me.
You keep me safe, and I always trust you.

—

PSALM 25:1–2a, 4–5

Today I trust only in the Lord, and I give God my heart.

You, Lord, are the light that keeps me safe. I am not afraid of anyone. You protect me, and I have no fears.

—

PSALM 27:1

Today the light of God shines through me.

I ask only one thing, Lord: Let me live in your house every day of my life to see how wonderful you are and to pray in your temple.

—

PSALM 27:4

Today I open my mind to the never-ending outpouring of the Holy Spirit's bountiful blessings.

You have turned my mourning into joyful dancing. You have taken away my clothes of mourning and clothed me with joy, that I might sing praises to you and not be silent. O Lord my God, I will give you thanks forever!

—

PSALM 30:11–12

Today I give thanks for all that God has given me.

I asked the Lord for help, and he saved me from all my fears. Keep your eyes on the Lord! You will shine like the sun and never blush with shame.

—

PSALM 34:4–5

Today I align my mind with the mind of God.

Your love is a treasure, and everyone finds shelter in the shadow of your wings. You give your guests a feast in your house, and you serve a tasty drink that flows like a river. The life-giving fountain belongs to you, and your light gives light to each of us.

—

PSALM 36:7–9

Today I find shelter in the house of the Lord.

I patiently waited, Lord, for you to hear my prayer. You listened and pulled me from a lonely pit full of mud and mire. You let me stand on a rock with my feet firm, and you gave me a new song, a song of praise to you. Many will see this, and they will honor and trust you, the Lord God.

—

PSALM 40:1–3

Today I give praise to God for all that He has done for me.

You, Lord God, have done many wonderful things, and you have planned marvelous things for us. No one is like you!

—

PSALM 40:5A

Today is a day of marvelous surprises from God.

Sacrifices and offerings are not what please you; gifts and payment for sin are not what you demand. But you made me willing to listen and obey. And so, I said, "I am here to do what is written about me in the book, where it says, 'I enjoy pleasing you. Your Law is in my heart.'"

—

PSALM 40:6–8

Today I will enjoy pleasing the Lord.

As a deer gets thirsty for streams of water, I truly am thirsty for you, my God. In my heart, I am thirsty for you, the living God.

—

PSALM 42:1–2A

Today my thirst for God is quenched by love.

Send your light and your truth to guide me. Let them lead me to your house on your sacred mountain.

—

PSALM 43:3

Today the light and truth of God guide me.

God is our mighty fortress, always ready to help in times of trouble. And so, we won't be afraid! Let the earth tremble and the mountains tumble into the deepest sea. The Lord All-Powerful is with us.

—

PSALM 46:1–2, 7A

Today I will not be afraid since I know God is all-powerful.

Help me to speak, and I will praise you, Lord. Offerings and sacrifices are not what you want. The way to please you is to feel sorrow deep in our hearts. This is the kind of sacrifice you won't refuse.

—

PSALM 51:15–17

Today I am set free by forgiving others and myself.

Please listen, God, and answer my prayer! I feel hopeless, and I cry out to you from a faraway land. Lead me to the mighty rock high above me. Let me live with you forever and find protection under your wings, my God.

—

Psalm 61:1–2, 4

Today I know that God can hear every word of my heart.

Only God gives inward peace,
and I depend on him.

—

PSALM 62:5

Today inner peace is mine.

I heard God say two things:
"I am powerful, and I am very kind."

—

PSALM 62:11–12A

Today the power of God fills me, and the kindness of
God washes over me.

You are my God. I worship you.
In my heart, I long for you,
as I would long for a stream in a scorching desert.

—

PSALM 63:1

Today I long for God, and know that God answers my call.

Make your promises to the Lord your God and do what you promise.

—

PSALM 76:11A

Today I make and keep my promises to God.

God will command his angels to protect you wherever you go.

—

PSALM 91:11

Today the angels of God surround me.

It is wonderful each morning to tell about your love
and at night to announce how faithful you are.

—

PSALM 92:2

Today I am faithful to Spirit morning, noon, and night.

Sing a new song to the Lord! Great is the Lord!
He is most worthy of praise!

—

PSALM 96:1A, 4A

Today God's greatness is my inspiration and my rock.

You, Lord, have saved my life from death, my eyes from tears, my feet from stumbling. Now I will walk at your side in this land of the living.

—

PSALM 116:8–9

Today I am alive anew, and walk with God in my heart.

Υου, Lord, are my choice, and I will obey you.

—

PSALM 119:57

Today everything I say and do is put into sacred action
and reaps sacred result.

I raise my eyes toward the mountains. Where will my help come from? My help comes from the Lord, the Maker of heaven and earth.

—

Psalm 121:1–2

Today I expect and experience help
from the Maker of heaven and earth.

Unless the Lord builds a house,
its builders labor over it in vain.

—

PSALM 127:1A

Today my very life is built upon the solid foundation of God.

Lord, my heart is not proud; my eyes are not haughty. I don't concern myself with matters too great or awesome for me. But I have stilled and quieted myself, just as a small child is quiet with its mother. Yes, like a small child is my soul within me.

—

PSALM 131:1–2

Today I am focused only on what God wants from me.

On the day I called, You answered me;
You increased strength within me.

—

PSALM 138:3

Today my strength is renewed and magnified by the Lord.

Where can I go from your Spirit? Or where can I flee from your presence? If I ascend into heaven, You are there; if I make my bed in hell, behold, You are there. If I take the wings of the morning, and dwell in the uttermost parts of the sea, even there Your hand shall lead me, and Your right hand shall hold me.

—

PSALM 139:7–10

Today I know that no matter what my life looks like or where I go, God is here with me.

If I say, "Surely the darkness will hide me, and the light around me will become night"—even the darkness is not dark to You. The night shines like the day; darkness and light are alike to You.

—

PSALM 139:11–12

Today I know that no darkness can hide me, and that all darkness turns to God's light.

I will praise You, because I have been remarkably and wonderfully made. Your works are wonderful, and I know this very well.

—

PSALM 139:14

Today I realize that the Divine sees me as wonderfully made, so I can, too.

How precious are your thoughts concerning me, O God! How vast in number they are! If I try to count them, there would be more of them than there are grains of sand. When I wake up, I am still with you.

—

PSALM 139:17–18

Today I know that God knows me completely, and loves me infinitely.

The Lord supports everyone who falls.
He straightens the backs of those who
are bent over.

—

PSALM 145:14

Today I walk upright, knowing I am completely
supported by the Divine Spirit.

2009 ~ brother Billy Glenn Watson die

· march 29 ·

Let everything that breathes praise the Lord!
Hallelujah!

—

PSALM 150:6

Today my every breath praises God.

Trust the Lord with all your heart, and do not rely on your own understanding. In all your ways acknowledge him, and he will make your paths smooth.

—

PROVERBS 3:5–6

Today I trust completely, knowing that all that I need to know will be revealed to me.

Honor the Lord with your wealth and with the first and best part of all your income.

—

PROVERBS 3:9

Today I tithe my time, talent, and treasure to God.

God blesses everyone who has wisdom and common sense. Wisdom is worth more than silver; it makes you much richer than gold. Wisdom is more valuable than precious jewels; nothing you want compares with her.

—

PROVERBS 3:13–15

Today wisdom is my guide and common sense is my rule.

Carefully guard your thoughts because they are the source of true life.

—

PROVERBS 4:23

Today I weed the garden of my mind,
carefully choosing each thought.

· april 3 ·

Watching what you say can save you a lot of trouble. The right word at the right time is like precious gold set in silver.

—

PROVERBS 21:23; 25:11

Today every word I speak will be loving and kind and true.

Just as iron sharpens iron, friends sharpen the minds of each other.

—

PROVERBS 27:17

Today I give thanks for the blessing of my friends.

Every word of God is pure; He is a shield to those who put their trust in Him.

—

PROVERBS 30:5

Today I am protected by the shield of faith.

Everything on earth has its own time and its own season. There is a time for birth and death, planting and reaping, for killing and healing, destroying and building, for crying and laughing, weeping and dancing, for throwing stones and gathering stones, embracing and parting. There is a time for finding and losing, keeping and giving, for tearing and sewing, listening and speaking. There is also a time for love and hate, for war and peace.

—

ECCLESIASTES 3:1–8

Today I am in rhythm with the rhythm of life.

Two people can accomplish more than twice as much as one; they get a better return for their labor.

—

ECCLESIASTES 4:9

Today I help others and allow others to help me.

Be happy and enjoy eating and drinking! God decided long ago that this is what you should do.

—

ECCLESIASTES 9:7

Today happiness and joy are mine, in all that I do.

Whatever you do, do well.

—

ECCLESIASTES 9:10A

Today I commit myself to excellence in all that I do.

Words of wisdom spoken softly make much more sense than the shouts of a ruler to a crowd of fools.

—

ECCLESIASTES 9:17

Today I will speak my truth softly and firmly.

Cast your bread upon the waters,
for after many days you will find it again.

—

ECCLESIASTES 11:1

Today I know that God's timing is perfect in every way.

How beautiful you are, my darling,
how beautiful!

—

SONG OF SOLOMON 1:15A

Today I glory in the beauty of the Darling.

Love is as strong as death. Many waters cannot quench love; rivers cannot wash it away.

—

SONG OF SOLOMON 8:6–7

Today I will express love fully and freely.

Then I heard the voice of the Lord, saying,
"Whom shall I send. And who will go for us?"
And I said, "Here I am! Send me."

—

Isaiah 6:8

Today I say "yes" to whatever God has in store for me.

A highway will be there; it will be called the Way of Holiness.

—

ISAIAH 35:8A

Today I stay on the highway of the Divine,
knowing it leads me to where I need to go.

I will give you the treasures of darkness, riches stored in secret places, so that you may know that I am the Lord, the God of Israel, who summons you by name.

—

ISAIAH 45:3

Today I discover the beauty hidden beneath the pain.

I alone am God, the First and the Last.

—

ISAIAH 48:12B

Today I realize there is only One, and I live in that truth.

Behold, I have engraved you on the palms of my hands.

—

ISAIAH 49:16A

Today I know that I am never forgotten by God.

The rain and snow come down from the heavens and stay on the ground to water the earth. They cause the grain to grow, producing seed for the farmer and bread for the hungry. It is the same with my word. I send it out, and it always produces fruit. It will accomplish all I want it to, and it will prosper everywhere I send it.

—

ISAIAH 55:10–11

Today I know that every positive thought
will produce a positive result.

The Lord will guide you continually, giving you water when you are dry and restoring your strength. You will be like a well-watered garden, like an ever-flowing spring.

—

Isaiah 58:11

Today I know my search is over—I have found the everlasting God, who dwells within my heart.

No longer will you need the sun to shine by day, nor the moon to give its light by night, for the Lord your God will be your everlasting light, and your God will be your glory.

—

Isaiah 60:19

Today I see God reflected in every experience and every person.

We are the clay, and you are our potter.
We all are formed by your hand.

—

Isaiah 64:8

Today I allow God to form me into a vessel for good.

I will answer them before they even call to me.
While they are still talking about their needs,
I will go ahead and answer their prayers!

—

ISAIAH 65:24

Today I will know deeply that God answers my prayers
as I believe.

Before I formed you in the womb I knew you,
and before you were born I consecrated you.

—

JEREMIAH 1:5A

Today is the day that I realize how intimately God
knows me, and loves me.

If I tell you to go and speak to someone, then go! And when I tell you what to say, don't leave out a word! I promise to be with you and keep you safe, so don't be afraid.

—

JEREMIAH 1:7B–8

Today the Lord speaks through me, and I am unafraid.

Blessed is the man who trusts in the Lord, whose trust is the Lord. He is like a tree planted by water, that sends out its roots by the stream, and does not fear when heat comes, for its leaves remain green, and is not anxious in the year of drought, for it does not cease to bear fruit.

—

JEREMIAH 17:7–8

Today my trust is in God alone.

I will turn their mourning to joy, will comfort
them, and make them rejoice rather than sorrow.

—

JEREMIAH 31:13B

Today my sorrows turn to joys,
and I rejoice in the goodness of God.

I will write my laws on their hearts and minds.
I will be their God, and they will be my people.

—

JEREMIAH 31:33B

Today I use the laws of the Divine, knowing that as I
believe, so shall I receive.

I will make an everlasting covenant with them:
I will never stop doing good for them.

—

JEREMIAH 32:40A

Today I enter into a covenant with God,
dedicating everything I do to the One.

Call to me and I will answer you, and will tell you great and hidden things that you have not known.

—

JEREMIAH 33:3

Today I feel the warmth of the Divine Presence forever welling up from within me.

The steadfast love of the Lord never ceases; his mercies never come to an end; they are new every morning.

—

LAMENTATIONS 3:22–23A

Today is new, and I am newly awakened in it.

"The LORD is my portion," says my soul, "therefore I hope in Him." The LORD is good to those who wait for Him, to the soul who seeks Him.

—

LAMENTATIONS 3:24–25

Today my gratitude is overflowing.

You answered my prayer and came when I was in need. You told me, "Don't worry!"

—

LAMENTATIONS 3:56B–57

Today I will not worry about anything.

I will give them one heart, and a new spirit I will put within them. I will remove the heart of stone from their flesh and give them a heart of flesh.

—

Ezekiel 11:19

Today I proclaim my divine inheritance,
and allow my heart to be filled with God's good.

For I am the Lord; I will speak the word that I will speak, and it will be performed.

—

Ezekiel 12:25a

Today God's word in my heart will be made manifest.

My Spirit will give you breath,
and you will live again.

—

EZEKIEL 37:14A

Today the breath of God is breathing through me.

He reveals deep and secret things; He knows what is in the darkness, and light dwells with Him.

—

DANIEL 2:22

Today my darkness is turned to Light.

I prayed to God in heaven, and my mind was healed.

—

DANIEL 4:34A

Today my healing is made manifest in me.

He knelt down in prayer three times a day, giving thanks to God.

—

DANIEL 6:10B

Today I pray ceaselessly, giving thanks to God all day.

I am the one who answers your prayers and cares for you. I am like a tree that is always green; all your fruit comes from me.

—

HOSEA 14:8

Today I am strong in the power of the almighty God.

I will pour out my Spirit on all flesh.

—

JOEL 2:28B

Today Life speaks to me, and I listen.

Come back to me and live!

—

AMOS 5:4B

Today my life is full and rich and peaceful.

As you have done, it shall be done to you;
your deeds shall return on your own head.

—

Obadiah 15b

Today I am held in the goodness of the Lord.

I called out to the Lord in my great trouble,
and he answered me.

—

JONAH 2:2A

Today I speak with God, and I listen to His answer.

When my life was slipping away, I remembered you—and in your holy temple you heard my prayer.

—

JONAH 2:7

Today every good I have experienced is now increased and multiplied.

I will look to the Lord; I will wait for the God of my salvation; my God will hear me.

—

MICAH 7:7

Today I see the hand of God wherever I turn.

The Lord is good. He protects those who trust him in times of trouble.

—

NAHUM 1:7

Today I know the goodness of God in every area of my life.

Write the vision. . . . For still the vision awaits its appointed time; it hastens to the end—it will not lie. If it seems slow, wait for it; it will surely come; it will not delay.

—

HABAKKUK 2:2–3

Today God expresses His love for me through friendship, peace, and harmony.

The Lord your God wins victory after victory and is always with you. He celebrates and sings because of you, and he will refresh your life with his love.

—

ZEPHANIAH 3:17

Today I elevate my faith and walk in the rhythm of the Lord.

I am with you, says the Lord.

—

HAGGAI 1:13B

Today the Lord is revealed to me.

"Return to Me," says the Lord of hosts,
"and I will return to you."

—

ZECHARIAH 1:3

Today I return to the Lord.

"Try Me now in this," says the Lord of hosts, "If I will not open for you the windows of heaven and pour out for you such blessing that there will not be room enough to receive it."

—

MALACHI 3:10B

Today I open and receive all of God's riches in my life.

Blessed are the poor in spirit,
   for theirs is the kingdom of heaven.
Blessed are those who mourn, for they shall be comforted.
Blessed are the meek, for they shall inherit the earth.
Blessed are those who hunger and thirst for
   righteousness, for they shall be satisfied.
Blessed are the merciful, for they shall receive mercy.
Blessed are the pure in heart, for they shall see God.
Blessed are the peacemakers, for they shall be called
   sons of God.
Blessed are those who are persecuted for righteousness'
   sake, for theirs is the kingdom of heaven.

—

MATTHEW 5:3–10

Today I choose to identify myself with all that belongs
to truth, beauty, and peace.

You are the light of the world. A city set on a hill cannot be hidden. Nor do people light a lamp and put it under a basket, but on a stand, and it gives light to all in the house. In the same way, let your light shine before others, so that they may see your good works and give glory to your Father who is in heaven.

—

MATTHEW 5:14–16

Today I no longer allow myself to be a victim, and instead shine my light boldly.

I say to you, Love your enemies and pray for those who persecute you, so that you may be sons of your Father who is in heaven. For he makes his sun rise on the evil and on the good, and sends rain on the just and on the unjust. For if you love those who love you, what reward do you have?

—

MATTHEW 5:44–46A

Today I love and pray for those who have hurt me.

. . . lay up for yourselves treasures in heaven, where neither moth nor rust destroys and where thieves do not break in and steal. For where your treasure is, there your heart will be also.

—

MATTHEW 6:20–21

Today I know that joy is my treasure.

Which of you by being anxious can add a single hour to his span of life?

—

Matthew 6:27

Today I surrender all of my worries to God.

Therefore do not be anxious, saying, "What shall we eat?" or "What shall we drink?" or "What shall we wear?" For . . . your heavenly Father knows that you need them all. But seek first the kingdom of God and his righteousness, and all these things will be added to you.

—

MATTHEW 6:31–33

Today I seek the kingdom of God first,
and I believe in the promise of God.

Ask, and it will be given to you; seek, and you will find; knock, and it will be opened to you. For everyone who asks receives, and the one who seeks finds, and to the one who knocks it will be opened.

—

MATTHEW 7:7–8

Today I ask for what I need, and believe I will receive it.

So whatever you wish that others would do to you, do also to them, for this is the Law.

—

MATTHEW 7:12A

Today I pray for blessings for everyone in my life.

Behold, I am sending you out as sheep in the midst of wolves, so be wise as serpents and innocent as doves.

—

MATTHEW 10:16

Today I listen to that still small voice inside to guide me throughout the day.

. . . do not be anxious how you are to speak or what you are to say, for what you are to say will be given to you in that hour. For it is not you who speak, but the Spirit of your Father speaking through you.

—

MATTHEW 10:19–20

Today I allow the voice of my Creator to speak through me.

Come to me, all who labor and are heavy laden, and I will give you rest. Take my yoke upon you, and learn from me, for I am gentle and lowly in heart, and you will find rest for your souls. For my yoke is easy, and my burden is light.

—

MATTHEW 11:28–30

Today I give all of my burdens to God,
and I rest in God's grace.

For out of the abundance of the heart, the mouth speaks. The good person out of his good treasure brings forth good.

—

MATTHEW 12:34b–35a

Today I give to God and to others from my heart and my treasure.

The kingdom of heaven is like treasure hidden in a field, which a man found and covered up. Then in his joy he goes and sells all that he has and buys that field.

—

MATTHEW 13:44

Today I focus on the joy of Life.

Again, the kingdom of heaven is like a merchant in search of fine pearls, who, on finding one pearl of great value, went and sold all that he had and bought it.

—

MATTHEW 13:45–46

Today I devote to hearing what Life is trying to tell me, and then doing what it says.

. . . and they cried out in fear. But immediately Jesus spoke to them, saying, "Take heart; it is I. Do not be afraid."

—

MATTHEW 14:26B–27

Today I fear not, for the Lord is my God.

Jesus answered her, "O woman, great is your faith! Be it done for you as you desire."

—

MATTHEW 15:28A

Today I have faith that my word, in God's name, will not return to me unfulfilled.

For truly I say to you, if you have faith like a grain of mustard seed, you will say to this mountain, "Move from here to there," and it will move, and nothing will be impossible for you.

—

MATTHEW 17:20B

Today I nurture and grow the seed of my faith.

Truly, I say to you, unless you turn and become like children, you will never enter the kingdom of heaven. Whoever humbles himself like this child is the greatest in the kingdom of heaven.

—

MATTHEW 18:3–4

Today I move forward with a childlike spirit of trust, innocence, and awe.

Truly, I say to you, whatever you bind on earth shall be bound in heaven, and whatever you loose in earth shall be loosed in heaven.

—

MATTHEW 18:18

Today whatever has bound me in the past is loosened and I am set free.

If two of you agree on earth about anything they ask, it will be done for them by my Father in heaven. For where two or three are gathered in my name, there am I among them.

—

MATTHEW 18:19–20

Today I pray with a partner
and maximize the power of prayer.

With man this is impossible, but with God all things are possible.

—

MATTHEW 19:26B

Today I live in the possibilities of God, knowing that they are available to me.

Truly, I say to you, if you have faith and do not doubt . . . if you say to this mountain, "Be taken up and thrown into the sea," it will happen. And whatever you ask in prayer, you will receive, if you have faith.

—

MATTHEW 21:21–22

Today I draw close to the Divine at the center of my being, and rest in calm assurance.

You shall love the Lord your God with all your heart and with all your soul and with all your mind. This is the great and first commandment. And a second is like it: You shall love your neighbor as yourself.

—

MATTHEW 22:37–39

Today my love for God and for others floods through me.

Well done, good and faithful servant. You have been faithful over a little; I will set you over much.

—

MATTHEW 25:21

Today I am faithful to the One who created me, and faithful to my own soul.

And behold, I am with you always,
to the end of the age.

—

MATTHEW 28:20B

Today my life is an example of the love of God in action.

Follow me,
and I will make you become fishers of men.

—

MARK 1:17

Today I reach out to others with love.

Those that were sown on the good soil are the ones who hear the word and accept it and bear fruit, thirtyfold and sixtyfold and a hundredfold.

—

MARK 4:20

Today my thoughts, words, and actions are aligned with where my soul directs me.

Pay attention to what you hear: with the measure you use, it will be measured to you, and still more will be added to you. For to the one who has, more will be given, and from the one who has not, even what he has will be taken away.

—

MARK 4:24–25

Today I count all of my blessings,
and know that I live richly in the kingdom.

For whoever would save his life will lose it, but whoever loses his life for my sake and the gospel's will save it. For what does it profit a man to gain the whole world and forfeit his soul? For what can a man give in return for his soul?

—

MARK 8:35–37

Today everything in my mind and heart I give to God;
I withhold nothing.

All things are possible for one who believes.

—

MARK 9:23B

Today I accept the fullness of life from this moment on.

So you want first place? Then take the last place.
Be the servant of all.

—

MARK 9:35B

Today is God's day, and my heart is without fear.

Whoever receives one such child in my name receives me, and whoever receives me, receives not me but him who sent me.

—

MARK 9:37

Today I see the Divine in each and every person I meet.

Whatever you ask in prayer, believe that you have received it, and it will be yours.

—

MARK 11:24

Today I pray with confidence and gratitude.

Whenever you stand praying, forgive, if you have anything against anyone.

—

MARK 11:25A

Today I forgive anyone—including myself—who has harmed me.

Watch and pray that you may not enter into temptation.

—

MARK 14:38A

Today I do not give in to temptation,
but rather choose goodness.

My soul magnifies the Lord, and my spirit rejoices in God my Savior . . . for he who is mighty has done great things for me, and holy is his name.

—

LUKE 1:46–47, 49

Today the mighty God is magnified in all that I do
and say and believe.

You shall worship the Lord your God, and him only shall you serve.

—

LUKE 4:8B

Today, everywhere I go, is a day of worship in all that I do.

And no one puts new wine into old wineskins. If he does, the new wine will burst the skins and it will be spilled, and the skins will be destroyed. But new wine must be put into fresh wineskins.

—

LUKE 5:37–38

Today I am renewed and recommitted.

Blessed are you who are hungry now,
    for you shall be satisfied.
Blessed are you who weep now,
    for you shall laugh.

—

LUKE 6:21

Today my ears hear the whispers of Life urging me forward.

But I say to you who hear, Love your enemies, do good to those who hate you, bless those who curse you, pray for those who abuse you.

—

LUKE 6:27–28

Today I do not see anyone as an enemy, but rather as a teacher whom I can learn from and love.

As you wish that others would do to you,
do so to them.

—

Luke 6:31

Today I treat everyone as I would like to be treated.

Judge not, and you will not be judged; condemn not, and you will not be condemned; forgive, and you will be forgiven; give, and it will be given to you. Good measure, pressed down, shaken together, running over, will be put into your lap. For with the measure you use it will be measured back to you.

—

LUKE 6:37–38

Today my forgiveness opens me up to receive the blessings of the Spirit.

july 4

... each tree is known by its own fruit.

—

LUKE 6:44A

Today I realize that my good is at hand, and my
Redeemer lives within me.

The good person out of the good treasure of his heart produces good.

—

LUKE 6:45A

Today the Spirit refreshes me, and I can feel Him now, in each breath I take.

Your faith has saved you; go in peace.

—

LUKE 7:50B

Today the essence of Life Itself loves me and leads me.

For everyone who asks receives, and the one who seeks finds, and to the one who knocks it will be opened.

—

LUKE 11:10

Today I finally ask in faith for what my heart desires, and I receive in faith as well.

Are not five sparrows sold for two pennies? And not one of them is forgotten before God. Why, even the hairs of your heads are all numbered. Fear not; you are of more value than many sparrows.

—

LUKE 12:6–7

Today I know that I am a beloved child of God, who loves me exactly as I am.

Consider the lilies, how they grow: they neither toil nor spin, yet I tell you, even Solomon in all his glory was not arrayed like one of these. But if God so clothes the grass, which is alive in the field today, and tomorrow is thrown into the oven, how much more will he clothe you, O you of little faith!

—

LUKE 12:27–28

Today I know that all of my good comes to me from God.

Don't concern yourself about what you will eat or drink, and quit worrying about these things. Everyone in the world is concerned about these things, but your Father knows you need them. Rather, be concerned about his kingdom. Then these things will be provided for you.

—

LUKE 12:29–31

Today I concentrate on God's needs,
knowing that all of my needs are taken care of.

Don't be afraid, little flock.
Your Father is pleased to give you the kingdom.

—

LUKE 12:32

Today I accept all that the Father has in store for me,
and give thanks.

Everyone to whom much was given, of him much will be required, and from him to whom they entrusted much, they will demand the more.

—

LUKE 12:48B

Today I prove trustworthy of all that is given to me by Life.

Strive to enter through the narrow door.

—

LUKE 13:24A

Today I am on guard to make sure that my actions
match my intent.

Blessed is he who comes in the name of the Lord!

—

LUKE 13:35B

Today each moment is dedicated to the Lord.

For everyone who exalts himself will be humbled,
and he who humbles himself will be exalted.

—

LUKE 14:11

Today I am humbled by God's greatness.

One who is faithful in a very little is also faithful in much.

—

Luke 16:10a

Today I raise the bar of excellence in every area of my life.

You see, the kingdom of God is within you.

—

LUKE 17:21B

Today I get still, go within, and connect with my soul.

And he told them a parable to the effect that they ought always to pray and not lose heart.

—

LUKE 18:1

Today I begin and end the day with prayer.

Make up your minds not to worry beforehand how you will defend yourselves. For I will give you words and wisdom that none of your adversaries will be able to resist or contradict.

—

LUKE 21:14–15

Today I stay present in the present moment, and know that everything I need to do or say will be revealed to me.

And from his fullness we have all received, grace upon grace.

—

JOHN 1:16

Today I am filled with the grace of God.

PROTECT AGAINST SNAGGING

PLEASE BE MINDFUL WHEN WEARING
THIS JEWELRY WITH DELICATE
FABRICS AS SNAGGING COULD OCCUR.

www.stelladot.___.com

bed.

Today I walk in God's truth.

Whoever drinks of the water that I will give him will never be thirsty again. The water that I will give him will become in him a spring of water welling up to eternal life.

—

JOHN 4:14

Today I drink of the living waters of the Spirit.

God is spirit, and those who worship him must worship in spirit and truth.

—

JOHN 4:24

Today I worship the living God who has created all life.

Jesus said to them, "My food is to do the will of him who sent me and to accomplish his work."

—

JOHN 4:34

Today I remember that I am here to do my Father's business.

Do not labor for the food that perishes, but for the food that endures to eternal life.

—

JOHN 6:27A

Today I feast on the food of the Spirit.

Jesus said to them, "I am the bread of life; whoever comes to me shall not hunger, and whoever believes in me shall never thirst."

———

JOHN 6:35

Today I listen to Jesus' words, and I believe them.

It is the Spirit who gives life; the flesh is no help at all. The words that I have spoken to you are spirit and life.

—

JOHN 6:63

Today I rejoice and know that the Spirit gives me life.

If anyone thirsts, let him come to me and drink. Whoever believes in me, . . . "Out of his heart will flow rivers of living water."

—

JOHN 7:37B–38

Today the living water flows to me and through me.

I am the light of the world. Whoever follows me will not walk in darkness, but will have the light of life.

—

JOHN 8:12B

Today I walk in the Light.

I do nothing on my own authority, but speak just as the Father has taught me.

—

JOHN 8:28c

Today I go where God would have me go,
and do what God would have me do.

If you abide in my word, . . . you will know the truth, and the truth will set you free.

—

JOHN 8:31B–32

Today I live and breathe the truth, and I am free.

Whoever is of God hears the words of God.

—

JOHN 8:47A

Today I hear the word of God,
because I was created by God.

I came that they may have life and have it abundantly.

—

JOHN 10:10B

Today I live an abundant life,
giving and receiving with love.

I am the good shepherd. I know my own and my
own know me.

—

JOHN 10:14

Today I follow the Divine Shepherd.

My sheep hear my voice, and I know them, and they follow me. I give them eternal life, and they will never perish.

—

JOHN 10:27–28A

Today I hear the voice of the Eternal Song sing in my heart.

I am the resurrection and the life. Whoever believes in me, though he die, yet shall he live, and everyone who lives and believes in me shall never die. Do you believe this?

—

JOHN 11:25–26

Today I believe, and I live my belief fully.

I have come into the world as light, so that whoever believes in me may not remain in darkness.

—

JOHN 12:46

Today the light of God shines from me brighter than ever before.

A new commandment I give to you, that you love one another: just as I have loved you, you also are to love one another.

—

JOHN 13:34

Today my mind and my heart are filled with love for all who enter my world.

Let not your hearts be troubled. Believe in God; believe also in me.

—

JOHN 14:1

Today I give my troubles to God, and am free.

Truly, truly, I say to you, whoever believes in me will also do the works that I do; and greater works than these will he do.

—

JOHN 14:12A

Today the greatness of God is my greatness now.

Whatever you ask in my name, this I will do. If you ask me anything in my name, I will do it.

—

JOHN 14:13A, 14

Today all that I ask for that is in alignment with God is given to me.

I will ask the Father, and he will give you another
Helper, to be with you forever. . . . You know him,
for he dwells with you and will be in you.

—

JOHN 14:16, 17B

Today the Helper guides and lifts me at every turn, and
in every breath.

The Helper, the Holy Spirit, whom the Father will send in my name, he will teach you all things.

—

JOHN 14:26A

Today the Helper is my teacher, and I learn what Life has to teach me.

Peace I leave with you; my peace I give to you. Not as the world gives do I give to you. Let not your hearts be troubled, neither let them be afraid.

—

JOHN 14:27

Today I experience the peace that passes understanding.

I am the true vine, and my Father is the gardener.
He cuts off every branch in me that bears no fruit,
while every branch that does bear fruit he prunes so
that it will be even more fruitful.

—

JOHN 15:1–2

Today anything that is unnecessary in my life is let go.

I am the vine; you are the branches. Whoever abides in me and I in him, he it is that bears much fruit, for apart from me you can do nothing.

—

JOHN 15:5

Today I know that without God I can do nothing, and with God I can do everything.

If you abide in me, and my words abide in you, ask whatever you wish, and it will be done for you. By this my Father is glorified, that you bear much fruit.

—

JOHN 15:7–8A

Today I fulfill the will of God for me.

This is my commandment, that you love one another as I have loved you. Greater love has no one than this, that someone lay down his life for his friends.

———

JOHN 15:12–13

Today the great love of God flows from me and to everyone I meet.

If the people of this world hate you, just remember that they hated me first. If you belonged to the world, its people would love you. But you don't belong to the world. I have chosen you to leave the world behind, and this is why its people hate you.

—

JOHN 15:18–19

Today I do not belong to the world, but I belong to God.

When the Spirit of truth comes, he will guide you into all the truth, for he will not speak on his own authority, but whatever he hears he will speak, and he will declare to you the things that are to come.

—

John 16:13

Today I go to the silence within, and listen to the Spirit's direction.

All that the Father has is mine; therefore I said that he will take what is mine and declare it to you.

—

JOHN 16:15

Today I live in the beautiful bounty of the Lord.

Truly, truly, I say to you, whatever you ask of the Father in my name, he will give it to you. Until now you have asked nothing in my name. Ask, and you will receive, that your joy may be full.

—

JOHN 16:23B–24

Today my heart is filled with the joy of the Father.

I am not alone, for the Father is with me.

—

JOHN 16:32B

Today I realize that I do not take even one breath alone,
for God is always with me, breathing through me.

Sanctify them in the truth; your word is truth.

—

John 17:17

Today I am made new in the truth.

You have made known to me the paths of life; you will make me full of gladness with your presence.

—

ACTS 2:28

Today I walk the divine path to the life God intended for me.

And when they had prayed, the place in which they were gathered together was shaken, and they were all filled with the Holy Spirit and continued to speak the word of God with boldness.

Acts 4:31

Today the Spirit lives in me, as me, and through me.

We must obey God rather than men.

—

ACTS 5:29B

Today is for the Lord, and I praise God for life itself.

God is aware of your prayers and your gifts to the poor.

—

ACTS 10:4B

Today I am generous to others with my time and my treasures.

If you have any word of encouragement for the people, say it.

—

ACTS 13:15B

Today I am a force for positive change in the world.

For he did good by giving you rains from heaven and fruitful seasons, satisfying your hearts with food and gladness.

—

ACTS 14:17B

Today I come unto the Father and walk with Him.

The God who made the world and everything in it, being Lord of heaven and earth, does not live in temples made by man, nor is he served by human hands, as though he needed anything, since he himself gives to all mankind life and breath and everything.

—

Acts 17:24–25

Today each breath is the breath of God breathing in me.

In him we live and move and have our being,
. . . for we are indeed his offspring.

—

ACTS 17:28

Today I live and act as the child of the Creator of all life.

• september 1 •

2014 Charlotte awakens on

Do not be afraid, but go on speaking and do not
be silent, for I am with you.

—

ACTS 18:9B–10A

El Campo, Texas to find
JP dead, dying on the floor!

Today I am not afraid, and I speak from my heart.

The righteous shall live by faith.

—

ROMANS 1:17B

Today my journey leads me to the Spirit.

He will render to each one according to his works: to those who by patience in well-doing seek for glory and honor and immortality, he will give eternal life.

—

Romans 2:6–7

Today all that I do I do for the glory of God.

Therefore, since we have been justified by faith, we have peace with God.

—

ROMANS 5:1A

Today I give peace and I receive peace.

We rejoice in our sufferings, knowing that suffering produces endurance, and endurance produces character, and character produces hope, and hope does not put us to shame, because God's love has been poured into our hearts through the Holy Spirit who has been given to us.

—

ROMANS 5:3–5

Today I know that every experience only leads me back to God.

· september 6 ·

2010 - This book a gift from Jane! I give thanks you for the day Jane came into my life!

Now if we have died with Christ, we believe that we will also live with him. For the death he died he died to sin, once for all, but the life he lives he lives to God. So you also must consider yourselves dead to sin and alive to God in Christ Jesus.

—

ROMANS 6:8, 10–11

Today I am washed clean by God.

Those who live according to the Spirit set their minds on the things of the Spirit. To set the mind on the Spirit is life and peace.

—

ROMANS 8:5B, 6B

2010 - awake in Chicago, Zoo Convention! Thank You, God for the beauty of my life! I am so bless

Today I set my mind only on the Spirit.

2010
up-dress - b'fast @ Windows w/omelet & meat bus for
Lincoln Park 300 @ 8 30 a - Thank You, God, that for the
health that permits such a schedule!

• september 8 •

Those who are led by the Spirit of God are sons
of God. For you did not receive a spirit that makes
you a slave again to fear, but you received the Spirit
of sonship.

—

ROMANS 8:14–15A

Today I experience the freedom that God has intended for me.

Today we observe 50 years of married life! Thank Linda treats us to dinner @ PF Changs

We know that for those who love God all things
work together for good.

—

Romans 8:28a

Today I know that everything in my life is leading me to my good.

I give thanks & praise for this day!

• september 10 •

If God is for us, who can be against us?

—

ROMANS 8:31B

Today I don't see any enemies, only people to love.

Who shall separate us from the love of Christ? Shall tribulation, or distress, or persecution, or famine, or nakedness, or danger, or sword? No, in all these things we are more than conquerors through him who loved us. For I am sure that neither death nor life, nor angels, nor rulers, nor things present nor things to come, nor powers, nor height nor depth, nor anything else in all creation, will be able to separate us from the love of God in Christ.

—

ROMANS 8:35, 37–39A

Today I am one with the One.

For this very purpose I have raised you up, that I might show my power in you.

—

Romans 9:17a

Today I rise up above mediocrity and into greatness.

For the same Lord is Lord of all, bestowing his riches on all who call on him.

—

ROMANS 10:12B

Today I am rich in God.

If the root is holy, so are the branches.

—

ROMANS 11:16B

Today I know and believe that I was created
in the image of God.

• september 15 •

From him and through him and to him
are all things.

—

ROMANS 11:36A

Today is for God.

Do not conform any longer to the pattern of this world, but be transformed by the renewing of your mind. Then you will be able to test and approve what God's will is—his good, pleasing and perfect will.

—

ROMANS 12:2

Today my mind is renewed and I surrender myself to God's will for me.

Bless those who persecute you; bless and do not curse them. Rejoice with those who rejoice, weep with those who weep.

—

ROMANS 12:14–15

Today I bless everyone in my life, even those who do not wish me well.

Don't hit back; discover beauty in everyone. Don't insist on getting even; that's not for you to do. "I'll do the judging," says God. "I'll take care of it."

—

ROMANS 12:17, 19

Today I see beauty in everyone and everything I see.

Do not be overcome by evil, but overcome evil with good.

—

ROMANS 12:21

Today is good, and I rejoice in it.

Pay to all what is owed to them: taxes to whom taxes are owed, revenue to whom revenue is owed, respect to whom respect is owed, honor to whom honor is owed.

—

ROMANS 13:7

Today I settle my debts and move forward.

You shall love your neighbor as yourself. Love does no wrong to a neighbor; therefore love is the fulfilling of the law.

—

ROMANS 13:9B–10

Today I love my neighbor as myself.

The night is nearly over; the day is almost here. So let us put aside the deeds of darkness and put on the armor of light.

—

ROMANS 13:12

Today I wear the armor of light.

For if we live, we live to the Lord, and if we die, we die to the Lord. So then, whether we live or whether we die, we are the Lord's.

—

ROMANS 14:8

Today I live for the Lord.

For the kingdom of God is . . . righteousness and peace and joy in the Holy Spirit. So then let us pursue what makes for peace and for mutual upbuilding.

—

ROMANS 14:17, 19

Today I pursue peace and serve others.

Those of us who are strong and able in the faith need to step in and lend a hand to those who falter, and not just do what is most convenient for us. Strength is for service, not status. Each one of us needs to look after the good of the people around us, asking ourselves, "How can I help?"

—

ROMANS 15:1–2

Today I lend a helping hand to anyone who needs it.

Do you not know that you are God's temple and that God's Spirit dwells in you?

—

1 CORINTHIANS 3:16

Today I treat my body as a temple of God.

Just because something is technically legal doesn't mean that it's spiritually appropriate. If I went around doing whatever I thought I could get by with, I'd be a slave to my whims.

—

1 CORINTHIANS 6:12

Today my temptations have no control over me.

Each man has his own gift from God; one has this gift, another has that.

—

1 CORINTHIANS 7:7B

Today I use my God-given talent for good.

Only let each person lead the life that the Lord has assigned to him, and to which God has called him.

—

1 CORINTHIANS 7:17A

Today my life is an example of love, joy, and peace.

If anyone loves God, he is known by God.

—

1 CORINTHIANS 8:3

Today I proclaim my love for God in every thought,
word, and deed.

Remember that in a race everyone runs, but only one person gets the prize. You also must run in such a way that you will win.

—

1 Corinthians 9:24

Today I am excellent for God.

No temptation has seized you except what is common to man. And God is faithful; he will not let you be tempted beyond what you can bear. But when you are tempted, he will also provide a way out so that you can stand up under it.

—

1 CORINTHIANS 10:13

Today I know that I can bear all things, and that all things lead back to God.

Jane Roberts Stern b 1938/2011 11-19

So, whether you eat or drink, or whatever you do, do all to the glory of God.

—

1 CORINTHIANS 10:31

Today all that I do is for the glory of God.

Now there are varieties of gifts, but the same Spirit; and there are varieties of service, but the same Lord; and there are varieties of activities, but it is the same God who empowers them all in everyone.

—

1 Corinthians 12:4–6

Today the Spirit reveals to me new gifts.

To each is given the manifestation of the Spirit
for the common good.

—

1 Corinthians 12:7

Today my heart overflows with gratitude for my life.

For just as the body is one and has many members, and all the members of the body, though many, are one body, so it is with Christ. For in one Spirit we were all baptized into one body . . . and all were made to drink of one Spirit.

—

1 CORINTHIANS 12:12–13

Today I am molded and shaped by God.

If one member suffers, all suffer together; if one member is honored, all rejoice together.

—

1 CORINTHIANS 12:26

Today I give service to anyone who is suffering, and honor all I meet.

I may speak in the languages of humans and of angels. But if I don't have love, I am a loud gong or a clashing cymbal. I may have the gift to speak what God has revealed, and I may understand all mysteries and have all knowledge. I may even have enough faith to move mountains. But if I don't have love, I am nothing. I may even give away all that I have and give up my body to be burned. But if I don't have love, none of these things will help me.

—

1 CORINTHIANS 13:1–3

Today I embody love.

Love is patient. Love is kind. Love isn't jealous. It doesn't sing its own praises. It isn't arrogant. It isn't rude. It doesn't think about itself. It isn't irritable. It doesn't keep track of wrongs. It isn't happy when injustice is done, but it is happy with the truth. Love never stops being patient, never stops believing, never stops hoping, never gives up. Love never comes to an end.

—

1 Corinthians 13:4–8a

Today I use every experience as an opportunity to love more deeply.

When I was a child, I spoke and thought and reasoned as a child. But when I grew up, I put away childish things.

—

1 CORINTHIANS 13:11

Today I put away childish thoughts and habits, and grow up in my faith.

Now we see but a poor reflection as in a mirror; then we shall see face to face. Now I know in part; then I shall know fully, even as I am fully known.

—

1 CORINTHIANS 13:12

Today God knows me completely and loves me completely.

There are three things that will endure—faith, hope, and love—and the greatest of these is love.

—

1 Corinthians 13:13

Today my faith helps me to love more, and to give more.

Go after a life of love as if your life depended on it—because it does. Give yourselves to the gifts God gives you. Most of all, try to proclaim his truth.

—

1 Corinthians 14:1

Today I give my life to love, and to the gifts of God within me.

What am I to do? I will pray with my spirit, but I will pray with my mind also; I will sing praise with my spirit, but I will sing with my mind also.

—

1 Corinthians 14:15

Today my life is a prayer.

Dear brothers and sisters, don't be childish in your understanding of these things. Be innocent as babies when it comes to evil, but be mature in understanding matters of this kind.

—

1 CORINTHIANS 14:20

Today I pay attention to the wisdom of the Lord.

By the grace of God I am what I am, and His grace toward me was not in vain.

—

1 CORINTHIANS 15:10A

Today I live in the grace of God.

Do not be misled:
"Bad company corrupts good character."

—

1 CORINTHIANS 15:33

Today I guard my thoughts and my time.

Death is swallowed up in victory.
O death, where is your victory?
O death, where is your sting?

—

1 CORINTHIANS 15:54b–55

Today I will not fear death or change of any kind.

So, my dear brothers and sisters, be strong and steady, always enthusiastic about the Lord's work, for you know that nothing you do for the Lord is ever useless.

—

1 CORINTHIANS 15:58

Today I choose to be enthusiastic in all that I do.

Be on guard. Stand true to what you believe. Be courageous. Be strong. And everything you do must be done with love.

—

1 Corinthians 16:13–14

Today I stand true to what I believe.

Kym Watson
10.21.52 - 02.15.2013

He comforts us in all our troubles so that we can comfort others. When they are troubled, we will be able to give them the same comfort God has given us.

—

2 CORINTHIANS 1:4

Today I am comforted by God, and I in turn comfort others.

Indeed, we felt that we had received the sentence of death. But that was to make us rely not on ourselves but on God who raises the dead. He delivered us from such a deadly peril, and he will deliver us. On him we have set our hope that he will deliver us again.

—

2 Corinthians 1:9–10

Today I am delivered by God out of the depths and into the kingdom.

For all the promises of God find their Yes in him.
That is why it is through him that we utter our
Amen to God for his glory.

—

2 CORINTHIANS 1:20

Today I live God's YES.

You are a letter written not with ink but with the Spirit of the living God, a letter written not on tablets of stone but on tablets of human hearts.

—

2 CORINTHIANS 3:3B

Today my heart reveals the letter that God has written on it.

Wherever the Lord's Spirit is, there is freedom.

—

2 Corinthians 3:17b

Today my soul magnifies the love of the Lord.

We are pressed on every side by troubles, but we are not crushed and broken. We are perplexed, but we don't give up and quit. We are hunted down, but God never abandons us. We get knocked down, but we get up again and keep going.

—

2 CORINTHIANS 4:8–9

Today nothing keeps me down;
I keep rising and walking on.

We're not giving up. How could we! Even though on the outside it often looks like things are falling apart on us, on the inside, where God is making new life, not a day goes by without his unfolding grace.

—

2 CORINTHIANS 4:16

Today I persevere, nothing can stop me from doing what I am meant to do.

For our present troubles are quite small and won't last very long. Yet they produce for us an immeasurably great glory that will last forever! So we don't look at the troubles we can see right now; rather, we look forward to what we have not yet seen. For the troubles we see will soon be over, but the joys to come will last forever.

—

2 CORINTHIANS 4:17–18

Today I focus not on my problems, but on God's solutions.

God has prepared us for this and has given us his Spirit to guarantee it.

—

2 CORINTHIANS 5:5

Today I use prayer as my first resource, not my last resort.

For we walk by faith, not by sight.

—

2 Corinthians 5:7

Today I see through the lens of my soul.

If anyone is in Christ, he is a new creation; the old has gone, the new has come!

—

2 CORINTHIANS 5:17

Today is new, and I am newly awakened in it.

For we are the temple of the living God.

—

2 CORINTHIANS 6:16B

Today my mind is a temple, and I only allow the highest thoughts to dwell in it.

Give whatever you can according to what you have. If you are really eager to give, it isn't important how much you are able to give. God wants you to give what you have, not what you don't have.

—

2 Corinthians 8:11b–12

Today I give from my heart with open hands.

Remember this—a farmer who plants only a few seeds will get a small crop. But the one who plants generously will get a generous crop.

—

2 CORINTHIANS 9:6

Today I trade stinginess and tightfistedness for generosity.

You must each make up your own mind as to how much you should give. Don't give reluctantly or in response to pressure. For God loves the person who gives cheerfully. And God will generously provide all you need. Then you will always have everything you need and plenty left over to share with others.

—

2 CORINTHIANS 9:7–8

Today I decide to give without reservation or fear.

For though we live in the world, we do not wage war as the world does. The weapons we fight with are not the weapons of the world. On the contrary, they have divine power to demolish strongholds.

—

2 CORINTHIANS 10:3–4

Today I stand for peace without exception.

Be cheerful. Keep things in good repair. Keep your spirits up. Think in harmony. Be agreeable. Do all that, and the God of love and peace will be with you for sure.

2 CORINTHIANS 13:11

Today my positivity is infectious to all those around me.

For am I now trying to win the favor of people, or God?

—

GALATIANS 1:10A

Today I experience God's amazing grace.

Formerly, when you did not know God, you were enslaved to those that by nature are not gods. But now that you have come to know God, or rather to be known by God, how can you turn back again to the weak and worthless elementary principles of the world, whose slaves you want to be once more?

—

GALATIANS 4:8–9

Today I worship no other god but the one God.

A little yeast spreads through the whole batch of dough.

—

GALATIANS 5:9

Today I bring joy and laughter to all who are in my path.

It is absolutely clear that God has called you to a free life. Just make sure that you don't use this freedom as an excuse to do whatever you want to do and destroy your freedom. Rather, use your freedom to serve one another in love; that's how freedom grows. For everything we know about God's Word is summed up in a single sentence: Love others as you love yourself. That's an act of true freedom.

—

GALATIANS 5:13–14

Today I develop the freedom that God gave me,
and use it for good in the world.

The fruit of the Spirit is love, joy, peace, patience, kindness, goodness, faithfulness, gentleness, self-control; against such things there is no law.

—

GALATIANS 5:22–23

Today I choose love, joy, peace, patience, kindness, goodness, faithfulness, gentleness, and self-control in all areas of my life.

If we live by the Spirit, let us also walk by the Spirit.

—

GALATIANS 5:25

Today every step I take brings me closer and closer to God.

Don't get tired of doing what is good. Don't get discouraged and give up, for we will reap a harvest of blessing at the appropriate time.

—

GALATIANS 6:9

Today I get a second wind, and my strength is renewed.

I urge you to live a life worthy of the calling you have received. Be completely humble and gentle; be patient, bearing with one another in love. Make every effort to keep the unity of the Spirit through the bond of peace.

—

EPHESIANS 4:1–3

Today my life is an example of a life worth living.

Don't use foul or abusive language. Let everything you say be good and helpful, so that your words will be an encouragement to those who hear them.

—

Ephesians 4:29

Today I speak words that uplift, not tear down.

Be strong with the Lord's mighty power.

—

EPHESIANS 6:10B

Today the power and might of the Lord flows into my life.

That energy is God's energy, an energy deep within you, God himself willing and working at what will give him the most pleasure.

—

PHILIPPIANS 2:12–13

Today I am energized with joy.

In everything you do, stay away from complaining and arguing, so that no one can speak a word of blame against you. You are to live clean, innocent lives as children of God in a dark world. Let your lives shine brightly before them.

—

PHILIPPIANS 2:14–15

Today I am thankful for everything and have no complaints whatsoever.

Celebrate God all day, every day.
I mean, revel in him!

—

PHILIPPIANS 4:4

Today I delight in God's grand design, and my place in it.

Whatever is true, whatever is honorable, whatever is just, whatever is pure, whatever is lovely, whatever is commendable, if there is any excellence, if there is anything worthy of praise, think about these things. . . . Practice these things ·and the God of peace will be with you.

—

PHILIPPIANS 4:8, 9B

Today my mind dwells on high.

In any and every circumstance, I have learned the secret of facing plenty and hunger, abundance and need. I can do all things through him who strengthens me.

—

Philippians 4:12b–13

Today I know that the more I give the more I receive—
I give and receive freely.

Set your minds on things above, not on earthly things.

—

COLOSSIANS 3:2

Today I am filled with a spirit of gladness.

Work willingly at whatever you do, as though you were working for the Lord rather than for people.

—

COLOSSIANS 3:23

Today I am filled with an expectancy of good things.

You're sons of Light, daughters of Day. We live under wide open skies and know where we stand. So let's not sleepwalk through life like those others. Let's keep our eyes open and be smart.

—

1 Thessalonians 5:5–6

Today the energy of Life flows through me.

Be cheerful no matter what; pray all the time; thank God no matter what happens.

—

1 Thessalonians 5:16–17

Today is God's day in which I live and in which I greatly rejoice.

Our God gives you everything you need, makes you everything you're to be.

—

2 Thessalonians 1:2

Today the unerring wisdom of the Divine directs my way.

Since everything God created is good, we should not reject any of it. We may receive it gladly with thankful hearts. For we know it is made holy by the word of God and prayer.

—

1 TIMOTHY 4:4–5

Today I reject nothing, knowing that everything leads to my good.

Have nothing to do with irreverent, silly myths. Rather train yourself for godliness; for while bodily training is of some value, godliness is of value in every way.

—

1 Timothy 4:7–8a

Today my thoughts are radiant with the light of God.

A devout life does bring wealth, but it's the rich simplicity of being yourself before God.

—

1 Timothy 6:6

Today I am guided into right action, into happiness, and into success.

God has not given us a spirit of fear and timidity, but of power, love, and self-discipline.

—

2 TIMOTHY 1:7

Today God illumines my path and makes straight the way before me.

In a well-furnished kitchen there are not only crystal goblets and silver platters, but waste cans and compost buckets—some containers used to serve fine meals, others to take out the garbage. Become the kind of container God can use to present any and every kind of gift to his guests for their blessing.

—

2 TIMOTHY 2:20–21

Today I am a container for God, and am filled with God.

To the pure, all things are pure, but to the defiled and unbelieving, nothing is pure.

—

TITUS 1:15A

Today I know that everything in my life is led by the action of Truth and Love.

The grace of the Lord Jesus Christ be with your spirit.

—

PHILEMON 25

Today I am compelled to move in the right direction,
to know what to do, and how best to do it.

Nothing in all creation is hidden from God's sight. Everything is uncovered and laid bare before the eyes of him to whom we must give account.

—

HEBREWS 4:13

Today everything in my life is revealed to God, and I am loved and forgiven.

We who have run for our very lives to God have every reason to grab the promised hope with both hands and never let go.

—

HEBREWS 6:18

Today I hold on tightly to God's promises,
and let them be my comfort.

We are not of those who shrink back and are destroyed, but of those who have faith and preserve their souls.

—

HEBREWS 10:39

Today I know that I give back the best that is in me.

What is faith? It is the confident assurance that what we hope for is going to happen. It is the evidence of things we cannot yet see.

—

HEBREWS 11:1

Today I know that the Spirit goes before me and makes perfect, plain, direct, and immediate my way.

By faith we understand that the universe was created by the word of God, so that what is seen was not made out of things that are visible.

—

HEBREWS 11:3

Today I am calm, and live in absolute certainty that God leads my way.

As you endure this divine discipline, remember that God is treating you as his own children.

—

Hebrews 12:7a

Today the peace of God is at the center of my being.

God is not an indifferent bystander. He's actively cleaning house, torching all that needs to burn, and he won't quit until it's all cleansed. God himself is Fire!

—

HEBREWS 12:28–29

Today the house of my life is cleaned and cleared so that only God remains.

Whenever trouble comes your way, let it be an opportunity for joy. For when your faith is tested, your endurance has a chance to grow. So let it grow, for when your endurance is fully developed, you will be strong in character and ready for anything.

—

JAMES 1:2–4

Today I realize that change always brings opportunity.

If you need wisdom—if you want to know what God wants you to do—ask him, and he will gladly tell you. But when you ask him, be sure that you really expect him to answer, for a doubtful mind is as unsettled as a wave of the sea that is driven and tossed by the wind.

—

JAMES 1:5–6

Today I accept what the Lord brings me, knowing that no matter how it looks it is a gift.

Be doers of the word, and not hearers only.

—

JAMES 1:22

Today I take positive and powerful action.

Do you think you'll get anywhere in this if you learn all the right words but never do anything? Does merely talking about faith indicate that a person really has it?

—

JAMES 2:14

Today I permit authenticity and integrity to enter my soul and my actions.

The wisdom that comes from heaven is first of all pure. It is also peace loving, gentle at all times, and willing to yield to others. It is full of mercy and good deeds. It shows no partiality and is always sincere. And those who are peacemakers will plant seeds of peace and reap a harvest of goodness.

—

JAMES 3:17–18

Today there is nothing but peace, and I bring this peace into my life experience.

Get down on your knees before the Master;
it's the only way you'll get on your feet.

—

JAMES 4:10

Today I meet every doubt that enters my mind with
confident faith.

Don't repay evil for evil. Don't retaliate when people say unkind things about you. Instead, pay them back with a blessing. That is what God wants you to do, and he will bless you for it.

—

1 PETER 3:9

Today I start my day with peace and live my day in peace.

Can anyone really harm you for being eager to do good deeds?

—

1 Peter 3:13

Today I think upon whatever things are good and true.

Be humble in the presence of God's mighty power, and he will honor you when the time comes. God cares for you, so turn all your worries over to him.

—

1 Peter 5:6–7

Today I live in the Divine Presence.

Do your best to improve your faith . . . by adding goodness, understanding, self-control, patience, devotion to God, concern for others, and love.

—

2 Peter 1:5–7

Today I live and move and have my being in God.

The Lord is not slow to fulfill his promise as some count slowness, but is patient toward you.

—

2 PETER 3:9A

Today I am governed by God's timing, and I know I am always in the right place at the right time.

God is light, and in him is no darkness at all.

—

1 JOHN 1:5B

Today every atom of my being radiates health and vitality and love.

Anyone who claims to live in God's light and hates a brother or sister is still in the dark. It's the person who loves brother and sister who dwells in God's light and doesn't block the light from others.

—

1 John 2:9–10

Today I share my good with others.

Don't love the world's ways. Don't love the world's goods. Love of the world squeezes out love for the Father.

—

1 JOHN 2:15

Today I completely surrender myself to the One.

What marvelous love the Father has extended to us! Just look at it—we're called children of God! That's who we really are.

—

1 JOHN 3:1

Today I realize that God is my only reality, and He dwells in me.

Every child of God can defeat the world, and our faith is what gives us this victory.

—

1 JOHN 5:4

Today I know that every apparent defeat is a chance for resurrection.

Love means doing what God has commanded us, and he has commanded us to love one another, just as you heard from the beginning.

—

2 JOHN 6

Today the perfect law of good is operating through me.

Watch out, so that you do not lose the prize for which you have been working so hard. Be diligent so that you will receive your full reward.

—

2 JOHN 8

Today I exult in God's abundant life.

Never follow a bad example, but keep following the good one; whoever does what is right is from God, but no one who does what is wrong has ever seen God.

—

3 JOHN 11

Today the good I realize for myself I realize for all others.

Relax, everything's going to be all right; rest, everything's coming together; open your hearts, love is on the way!

—

JUDE 2

Today I rest in divine assurance and divine security.

I am the Alpha and the Omega, the beginning and the end. To the thirsty I will give from the spring of the water of life without payment.

—

REVELATION 21:6

Today I live in the life of God, and I give thanks.

my favorite verses

translation guide

In creating this book, we used nine translations, going through the book verse by verse, translation by translation, to make sure we found the translation for each verse that we felt was the clearest and easiest to use. We encourage you to read through favorite verses in each of the translations (and other translations that we didn't use) to find the versions that work best for you.

TRANSLATIONS USED

ESV – English Standard Version

NIV – New International Version

NLT – New Living Translation

The Message

NKJV – New King James Version

CEV – Contemporary English Version

HSCB – Holman Christian Standard Bible

NJB – New Jerusalem Bible

God's Word – God's Word Translation

January 1 – ESV	February 7 – ESV	March 15 – CEV	April 21 – NLT
January 2 – NLT	February 8 – CEV	March 16 – CEV	April 22 – NLT
January 3 – NKJV	February 9 – NIV	March 17 – NLT	April 23 – NLT
January 4 – NLT	February 10 – NLT	March 18 – CEV	April 24 – ESV
January 5 – NKJV	February 11 – NIV	March 19 – CEV	April 25 – CEV
January 6 – CEV	February 12 – NLT	March 20 – HSCB	April 26 – ESV
January 7 – CEV	February 13 – CEV	March 21 – HSCB	April 27 – NKJV
January 8 – ESV	February 14 – CEV	March 22 – NLT	April 28 – CEV
January 9 – NIV	February 15 – ESV	March 23 – HSCB	April 29 – NLT
January 10 – NKJV	February 16 – NKJV	March 24 – NKJV	April 30 – ESV
January 11 – NIV	February 17 – CEV	March 25 – HCSB	May 1 – ESV
January 12 – NIV	February 18 – CEV	March 26 – HCSB	May 2 – NKJV
January 13 – NIV	February 19 – CEV	March 27 – God's Word	May 3 – CEV
January 14 – NLT	February 20 – CEV	March 28 – God's Word	May 4 – ESV
January 15 – NLT	February 21 – CEV	March 29 – God's Word	May 5 – ESV
January 16 – NIV	February 22 – NKJV	March 30 – God's Word	May 6 – CEV
January 17 – NIV	February 23 – NKJV	March 31 – God's Word	May 7 – NKJV
January 18 – NKJV	February 24 – NKJV	April 1 – CEV	May 8 – CEV
January 19 – The Message	February 25 – NKJV	April 2 – CEV	May 9 – CEV
January 20 – NLT	February 26 – CEV	April 3 – CEV	May 10 – NLT
January 21 – CEV	February 27 – CEV	April 4 – CEV	May 11 – NKJV
January 22 – ESV	February 28 – CEV	April 5 – NKJV	May 12 – NLT
January 23 – ESV	February 29 – NLT	April 6 – CEV	May 13 – ESV
January 24 – NLT	March 1 – CEV	April 7 – NLT	May 14 – NLT
January 25 – God's Word	March 2 – CEV	April 8 – CEV	May 15 – CEV
January 26 – NLT	March 3 – CEV	April 9 – NLT	May 16 – NKJV
January 27 – NLT	March 4 – CEV	April 10 – CEV	May 17 – CEV
January 28 – CEV	March 5 – CEV	April 11 – NIV	May 18 – ESV
January 29 – CEV	March 6 – CEV	April 12 – NLT	May 19 – CEV
January 30 – ESV	March 7 – CEV	April 13 – NIV	May 20 – NKJV
January 31 – ESV	March 8 – CEV	April 14 – NIV	May 21 – NKJV
February 1 – CEV	March 9 – CEV	April 15 – NIV	May 22 – NKJV
February 2 – God's Word	March 10 – CEV	April 16 – NIV	May 23 – ESV
February 3 – ESV	March 11 – CEV	April 17 – NLT	May 24 – ESV
February 4 – CEV	March 12 – CEV	April 18 – ESV	May 25 – ESV
February 5 – CEV	March 13 – CEV	April 19 – NLT	May 26 – ESV
February 6 – CEV	March 14 – CEV	April 20 – NLT	May 27 – ESV

May 28 – ESV	July 4 – ESV	August 10 – ESV	September 16 – NIV
May 29 – ESV	July 5 – ESV	August 11 – ESV	September 17 – ESV
May 30 – ESV	July 6 – ESV	August 12 – ESV	September 18 – The Message
May 31 – ESV	July 7 – ESV	August 13 – ESV	September 19 – ESV
June 1 – ESV	July 8 – ESV	August 14 – NIV	September 20 – ESV
June 2 – ESV	July 9 – ESV	August 15 – ESV	September 21 – ESV
June 3 – ESV	July 10 – God's Word	August 16 – ESV	September 22 – NIV
June 4 – ESV	July 11 – God's Word	August 17 – ESV	September 23 – ESV
June 5 – ESV	July 12 – ESV	August 18 – CEV	September 24 – ESV
June 6 – ESV	July 13 – ESV	August 19 – ESV	September 25 – The Message
June 7 – ESV	July 14 – ESV	August 20 – ESV	September 26 – ESV
June 8 – ESV	July 15 – ESV	August 21 – ESV	September 27 – The Message
June 9 – ESV	July 16 – ESV	August 22 – ESV	September 28 – NIV
June 10 – ESV	July 17 – God's Word	August 23 – ESV	September 29 – ESV
June 11 – ESV	July 18 – ESV	August 24 – ESV	September 30 – ESV
June 12 – ESV	July 19 – NIV	August 25 – ESV	October 1 – NLT
June 13 – ESV	July 20 – ESV	August 26 – ESV	October 2 – NIV
June 14 – ESV	July 21 – ESV	August 27 – God's Word	October 3 – ESV
June 15 – ESV	July 22 – ESV	August 28 – ESV	October 4 – ESV
June 16 – ESV	July 23 – ESV	August 29 – ESV	October 5 – ESV
June 17 – ESV	July 24 – ESV	August 30 – ESV	October 6 – ESV
June 18 – ESV	July 25 – ESV	August 31 – ESV	October 7 – ESV
June 19 – ESV	July 26 – ESV	September 1 – ESV	October 8 – God's Word
June 20 – ESV	July 27 – ESV	September 2 – ESV	October 9 – God's Word
June 21 – ESV	July 28 – ESV	September 3 – ESV	October 10 – NLT
June 22 – The Message	July 29 – ESV	September 4 – ESV	October 11 – NIV
June 23 – ESV	July 30 – ESV	September 5 – ESV	October 12 – NLT
June 24 – ESV	July 31 – ESV	September 6 – ESV	October 13 – The Message
June 25 – ESV	August 1 – ESV	September 7 – ESV	October 14 – ESV
June 26 – ESV	August 2 – ESV	September 8 – NIV	October 15 – NLT
June 27 – ESV	August 3 – ESV	September 9 – ESV	October 16 – NKJV
June 28 – ESV	August 4 – ESV	September 10 – ESV	October 17 – NIV
June 29 – ESV	August 5 – ESV	September 11 – ESV	October 18 – ESV
June 30 – ESV	August 6 – ESV	September 12 – ESV	October 19 – NLT
July 1 – ESV	August 7 – ESV	September 13 – ESV	October 20 – NLT
July 2 – ESV	August 8 – ESV	September 14 – ESV	October 21 – NLT
July 3 – ESV	August 9 – ESV	September 15 – ESV	October 22 – ESV

October 23 – ESV	November 16 – NLT	December 10 – The Message
October 24 – God's Word	November 17 – God's Word	December 11 – NLT
October 25 – God's Word	November 18 – NLT	December 12 – NLT
October 26 – NLT	November 19 – The Message	December 13 – ESV
October 27 – The Message	November 20 – ESV	December 14 – The Message
October 28 – NLT	November 21 – ESV	December 15 – NLT
October 29 – God's Word	November 22 – NIV	December 16 – The Message
October 30 – NKJV	November 23 – NLT	December 17 – NLT
October 31 – NIV	November 24 – The Message	December 18 – CEV
November 1 – NIV	November 25 – The Message	December 19 – CEV
November 2 – NLT	November 26 – The Message	December 20 – CEV
November 3 – NLT	November 27 – NLT	December 21 – ESV
November 4 – NLT	November 28 – ESV	December 22 – ESV
November 5 – NIV	November 29 – The Message	December 23 – The Message
November 6 – The Message	November 30 – NLT	December 24 – The Message
November 7 – HCSB	December 1 – The Message	December 25 – The Message
November 8 – ESV	December 2 – ESV	December 26 – CEV
November 9 – God's Word	December 3 – NLT	December 27 – NLT
November 10 – The Message	December 4 – NIV	December 28 – NLT
November 11 – ESV	December 5 – The Message	December 29 – NJB
November 12 – ESV	December 6 – ESV	December 30 – The Message
November 13 – NLT	December 7 – NLT	December 31 – ESV
November 14 – NIV	December 8 – ESV	
November 15 – NLT	December 9 – NLT	

permissions

ESV — English Standard Version
Scripture quotations are from The Holy Bible, English Standard Version, copyright © 2001 Crossway Bibles, a division of Good News Publishers. Used by permission. All rights reserved.

NIV — New International Version
Scriptures taken from the Holy Bible, New International Version®, NIV®. Copyright © 1973, 1978, 1984 by Biblica, Inc.™ Used by permission of Zondervan. All rights reserved worldwide.

NLT — New Living Translation
Scripture quotations marked NLT are taken from the Holy Bible, New Living Translation, copyright © 1996. Used by permission of Tyndale House Publisher, Inc., Wheaton, Illinois 60189. All rights reserved.

The Message
Scripture taken from THE MESSAGE. Copyright © 1993, 1994, 1995, 1996, 2000, 2001, 2002. Used by permission of NavPress Publishing Group.

NKJV — New King James Version
Scripture taken from the New King James Version. Copyright © 1982 by Thomas Nelson, Inc. Used by permission. All rights reserved.

CEV — Contemporary English Version
Scripture quotations marked CEV are taken from the Holy Bible, Contemporary English Version, copyright © 1995. Used by permission of the American Bible Society. All rights reserved.

HSCB — Holman Christian Standard Bible
Scripture quotations marked HCSB have been taken from the Holman Christian Standard Bible®, Copyright © 1999, 2000, 2002, 2003 by Holman Bible Publishers. Used by permission. Holman Christian Standard Bible®, Holman CSB®, and HCSB® are federally registered trademarks of Holman Bible Publishers.

NJB—New Jerusalem Bible.
Scriptural references are taken from the New Jerusalem Bible, published and copyright © 1985 by Darton, Longman & Todd Ltd. and Doubleday, a division of Random House Inc., and used by permission of the publishers.

God's Word — God's Word Translation
GOD'S WORD is a copyrighted work of God's Word to the Nations. Quotations are used by permission. Copyright © 1995 by God's Word to the Nations. All rights reserved.

about paraclete press

Who We Are

Paraclete Press is a publisher of books, recordings, and DVDs on Christian spirituality. Our publishing represents a full expression of Christian belief and practice—from Catholic to Evangelical, from Protestant to Orthodox.

We are the publishing arm of the Community of Jesus, an ecumenical monastic community in the Benedictine tradition. As such, we are uniquely positioned in the marketplace without connection to a large corporation and with informal relationships to many branches and denominations of faith.

What We Are Doing

Books | Paraclete publishes books that show the richness and depth of what it means to be Christian. Although Benedictine spirituality is at the heart of all that we do, we publish books that reflect the Christian experience across many cultures, time periods, and houses of worship. We publish books that nourish the vibrant life of the church and its people—books about spiritual practice, formation, history, ideas, and customs.

We have several different series, including the best-selling Living Library, Paraclete Essentials, and Paraclete Giants series of classic texts in contemporary English; A Voice from the Monastery—men and women monastics writing about living a spiritual life today; award-winning literary faith fiction and poetry; and the Active Prayer Series that brings creativity and liveliness to any life of prayer.

Recordings | From Gregorian chant to contemporary American choral works, our music recordings celebrate sacred choral music through the centuries. Paraclete distributes the recordings of the internationally acclaimed choir Gloriæ Dei Cantores, praised for their "rapt and fathomless spiritual intensity" by *American Record Guide*, and the Gloriæ Dei Cantores Schola, which specializes in the study and performance of Gregorian chant. Paraclete is also the exclusive North American distributor of the recordings of the Monastic Choir of St. Peter's Abbey in Solesmes, France, long considered to be a leading authority on Gregorian chant.

DVDs | Our DVDs offer spiritual help, healing, and biblical guidance for life issues: grief and loss, marriage, forgiveness, anger management, facing death, and spiritual formation.

Learn more about us at our Web site:
www.paracletepress.com, or call us toll-free at 1-800-451-5006.

You may also be interested in . . .

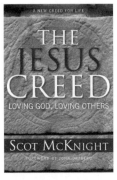

The Jesus Creed
ISBN: 978-1-55725-400-9 • $16.95, Paperback

"Make sure this new guide for living is on your shelf."
—Max Lucado

"Scot McKnight brings us into a conversation with Jesus
in the places and conditions in which we live
our ordinary lives." —Eugene Peterson

When an expert in the law asked Jesus for the greatest
commandment, Jesus gave his followers a new creed for life:
to love God with heart, soul, mind, and strength, and also to
love others as themselves. Discover how the Jesus Creed can
transform your life.

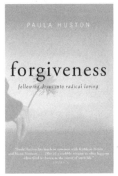

Forgiveness
Following Jesus into Radical Loving
ISBN: 978-1-55725-570-9 • $21.99, Hardcover

"In our broken world, forgiveness will ensure that evil
does not have the final word. This is a book of healing and
restitution, for those who need to accept forgiveness, and
for those who need to give it. I highly recommend it."
—Sr. Helen Prejean, author of *Dead Man Walking*

If you find it difficult to forgive or to accept forgiveness,
this book is your encouragement. With honesty and insight,
Paula Huston examines the intellectual, psychological, social,
and spiritual dimensions of forgiveness.

Available from Paraclete Press   www.paracletepress.com   1-800-451-5006